GALOS; Z J

THE VIVENOT ELEGIES

Along a Murmuring Brook

Lyric

Impressum

Bibliographical information of the German National Library.
The German National Library indexes this publication with the German National Bibliography. Detailed bibliographical data may be derived from the Internet website http://dnb.dnb.de

Producer and publisher: BoD-Books on Demand, Norderstedt

ISBN: 9783751919982

View towards Vivenot Lane

PROLOG

Originating from the first time of the realization of a quest for a return to his homeland, the poet has been inspired by R.M. Rilke's *Duino Elegies*, he read on the laptop of a friend. From a reasonable and affordable life in the South of Africa, he had also endeavoured with some art exhibitions of his creative work in Athens, Greece, besides, expressing his innerness in word and with his brush.

He had not intended returning from the natural wonders of exquisite beauty of the landscapes in the Karoo and the moonscape-appearances of Cape Agulhas, also the historically important city of Cape Town and the scenic drives along Chapman's Peak. A land of contrasts with a natural multitude of fauna and flora, of coloured earth and seas around its perimeter, semi-deserts and deserts in the western parts. A treasured gift of nature!

The legacy of rich decorated cave-walls and the culture of the San-people stayed as inspiration for ZG-the artist's major influence. Back to a Europe in the changing melting pot for a new civilization, due to a multitude of cultural migration, offered a new perspective. A trip back from Africa to one's roots, due to political changes that seemed to erode one's professional existence, is not an easy decision, very hurtful, but a necessary step for personal survival, especially at an ongoing age.

Into these contrasting events the basis of poetry and art of the poet and the artist has evolved as a healing dressing to the wounds inflicted by barbaric events and unnecessary violation; misunderstood freedom by the masses, a great mismanagement of ignorance and neglect of leadership, besides tribal leadership that had refused stubbornly to any change of its chiefdom's dominance.

However, having worked at various projects, including clinics, hospitals and cultural centres for all residents, irrespective of believe and colour, the artist's return to Europe has been disappointing, having worked as architect in South Africa, meeting suddenly with an unsurmountable local bureaucracy as the major hindrance for contributing - with one's experience of 30 years - to local projects.

Into this crass contrast of ability against bureaucracy, the artist's mind had generated an enormous boost for survival. ZJG, the poet has endeavoured to edit his poetry, short stories and novels, and offer them to a German Self-publishing agency for printing on demand. This welcome publishing company has furthered the incentive of the artist to publish his 'oeuvre complete' in due time. These elegies are an outcome of his time of resettlement, together with his spouse, into the countryside atmosphere near Vienna. In the ensuing solitude the artist turns productive in a welcome change of atmosphere as to the city of Vienna, a half-an hourly trip by public transport.

While he teaches German to an Egyptian immigrant, he is not surprised of the student's difficulties to integrate into the local society.

He meets a young woman-artist from Bangladesh at an exhibition and they become friends. He experiences the local art scene at the Academy of Fine Arts, where his friend is educated, and she shows him her work in progress that furthers his artistic experiences, while she brushes off her cultural legacy in her interesting work.

1.

Water Lane.

If I'd collapse of physical exhaustion

at this corner called Water Lane

descent to a murmuring brook

of a quaint forgotten village

who would find me

who'd come to my aid?

The wide-hipped angel of local

Info at an aged train station?

Or the fair-faced librarian at the

contemp museum of modern art?

The neighbour's partner taking

their dog for a walk

or the pale-faced lanky neighbour's son

who walks with a set of earphones

just like me?

A small path from the lower part of life

to the upper main road

high grass lining both sides

like a bed of flowers on a grave

a bed of comfort on the asphalt

darkened by a short stint of showers

quiet still baroque music

violin violoncello

into an early evening

clouded grey stripes of pink

the sleepy evening's call

at the end of the eighth month

when everybody sits for supper

TV/ laptop/ mobile phone activities

and I will cry out my pain

in another drawing

a new portrait of chance

a dot of paint from which

I grow a muse's face

from within a fading memory.

2.

Late evening at Top 5.

A common yard

late evening at top 5

the yard of no 35 and 37

off the mad traffic flow on

main street *Weidling*

where a heavy access gate had

been removed for easy access:

cars for the *Stakhanov-mechanic*

once a barrier against whistling sound

of growing through passing traffic

racing past the yard's collective ear.

The poet sits at his desk in a rectangular

kitchen

painting a journal of day and night dreams

lights at full blast-opposite at 37

with a lack of blinds or curtains

a woman's face with a small furry dog

she kisses tentatively

the dog with pricked ears lifts a paw

to greet?

The poet looking up at times as if he'd

notice in the dusk the presence of his

past muse

listening to OE1 radio

discussing a theme on sex.

The wish for sexual satisfaction

love and emotion - is good sex and

a penis – imagine!

be treated still as a taboo thing?

Sex workers are the teachers for

Good sexual knowledge. Hear!

Spurning the fantasy looking for

a sexual mate without running into

a wall of high emotional

confrontation:

you'll need a laptop my dear

the info-angel tells the poet

whereby the life of a man called ZZ

who lives victimized by his spouse's

bickering could be depicted.

Perhaps he is still not at ease

lacking a connection to society of

friendly Internet users/ sweethearts

friends and lovers.

Most people are afraid to out themselves.

Amazing that society still has a problem

with this theme: Sex and prostitution

for over four hundred years.

Listen to cool jazz - Miles Davis from

1940 when the poet heard its first sounds

just having been born. Black & White

smoky bars and the golden trumpet.

Jive talk and new sounds to play

gently it'll need a relaxed interpreter

to write a good poem –

you must be still cool.

Just like painting something with a new

kind of expression and approach.

Birth of the cool

birth of mystic realism

birth of contemporary art

presented by an artist in free expression

sounds that breathe out gentle or hard

while every night the opposite neighbour

of the poet

burns the midnight oil

shining on his manuscripts

neatly stacked in wall-covering shelves

this poet here at 35/5 has not yet

managed to afford and install

but he is working toward it: Books to

be accommodated from floor to desk

and above it a four-panel work on canvas

one design done already called:

Love' Sweep - Cool Art.

Hipster Age. Beatnik Age.

Age of Revolt

In the art of just existing

even more so at high age!

3.

Life's Surprises.

Life's surprises began to improve

the chain of little and monotonous

food lines

through discovery of a social market

close to famous food chains

of the greater players

who sponsor SOMA –

where thousands of socially disadvantaged

seek this unique market-run store for

basic food and with a reasonable variety

of products –

from milk vegetables and fruit

just on the verge of expiry dates and

to a tolerable more –

sweets, biscuits and vitamin beverages

with R's masterly command directed

but also showing a soft heart

in a toughened shell.

She offers the lonely poet a second hand

coffee maker - glorious filter coffee for the

poet to stay awake sitting day in and out

at his 80 x 100 working space.

for B it'll mean many cups a day

to shield her permanently sore head.

The poet is glad he can return from the

area of markets having spent a few bob

only and save on the fare for the bus

walking along a worked-out path ducking

through a busy crossroad intersection

to a series of pedestrian lanes

meandering along Weidling brook

to the centre of the village

dominated by the onion-shaped spire

of a baroque church and a local hall

where a museum/ a medical doctor

toilets and most important of all - a small

open library is located

where the writer in me may find some

interesting books of poetry romance and

stories about adventures/ love and travelling

even English books of short stories.

Along the way the child in me listens to music

through earphones connected to his mobile

phone perhaps a play or some repeated news.

Matinatta sung by a powerful tenor

who appeared at the Salzburg festivals?

what a voice! The tenor in me sings along

lifts me up to the wandering clouds

above the poet in me

above the artist in me

above my mortal shell

flying high over carefully laid out vineyards

and well-kept traditional homes

in art deco and in sezessionistic styles

of a rich cultural heritage

and bridges above the winding brook

above the confluences of smaller brooks

into the main one at the village close to

famous *Brunnenpark* villa with a fountain

and sculptures on its decorated façade.

The bypass to the narrow village road

which squeezes through the needle ear

at the historic church

and a street dedicated to *Nikolaus Lenau*

one of my favourite poets buried nearby.

Back and up *Vivenotweg* across the brook

along this pretty lane and the last bit of

incline called *Schredergasse*

to the entrance with the missing gate.

Woman & Dog in the Courtyard window

4.

The View.

Between the view –

restricted by the width of the tall window

from the poet's desk –

and the extensions of his perspective

along the meandering Weidling-brook

I wander along for a daily exercise

at the same time with the same speed

of gait

on the same walkway's light-grey

tarmac

but with different thoughts each time

over-crusting some familiar ones

which merge with the brook's continual

murmur

within its lined lush greens

below stone walls of well-kept estates

homes accessed via bridges

passed two gigantic wild chestnut trees

where neatly fresh cut stumps show

their terminated lives –

opposite home 21 –

where a golden girl with shoulder

touching hair's presence

disappeared into

on a Tuesday late afternoon

at my walking time

and I look out for her every day

but being Friday perhaps I have to wait

until Tuesday again to ask her for some

talking time.

And B calls me a Kantian scholar.

For now it's the seedless grapes B wanted

from Greece I'll carry home and taste a few

and they just might soothe her pains

perhaps. Perhaps.

I'll prefer travelling alone to Vienna

to buy some shoes and check out some shops

as I always know what I want

but also to avoid tiring discussions about taste

and a flurry of other emotional issues

we air as we want to do our own thing

our often opposed thing for our projection

of a future life.

Being together all of our lives we are still

close

yet living consciously mentally and physically

wide apart: In our different tastes

our contrasting preferred colour-schemes

in ways of living with our priorities

that are determined by the mood of fashion

for B. Fashionista.

While for me- the writer and poet it's a winding

road which will lead me to my goal of processing

my art on websites for sale

load my novels for online publication sites

while onto this day since Ana had been forced

to leave this blue planet

nobody else took much notice of the poet ZZ

in me nor the artist ZG

striving on another consciousness level

save for some friends in Greece/ Vienna/ Mexico

and also in the USA

in spite of numerous publications

in spite of having cried out to my guardian angel

and to the goddess of commercial success

but then in LOVE Aphrodite has been generous

and kind. I WRITE FOR LOVE.

I paint: LOVE & ART.

I write: APHRODITE ENCUMBERED Book I - V.

Waiting for more savings until the end of September

in order to purchase a *Travelmate*-laptop

continue to post the fruit of my creative mind.

5.

Nema.ameN

This morning is Saturday

thirtieth of August –

continual rain from *Weidling* to

Fünfhaus

bus to U-Bahn

finishing my trip at *PK's* shoe repair –

closed doors –

waiting in a sheltered entrance door

nearby

phone *PK* who has overslept

one well-repaired shoe in my holdall

back in the 58 tram

wet pants smelly raincoats

acid rain burns down one's face

took U6 to *Spittelau* but missed the

correct U4 had to switch trains at the

next station

Heiligenstadt in time for bus 238 to

Weidling and in a back seat Elena!

Best cook in these part of the scene

sat opposite to her

we talked and laughed

like some storybook's child sweethearts.

Exit at the *Weidling* station

we changed over to bus 241

and talked until her bus arrived.

I walked down to the traffic circle below

the train lines and up a steel stair

to the level of the four big market stores

the new area of local light industry.

Hood up in the rain toward the Soma

talked to R who asked me how the

coffeemaker was working she sold me

for a low price and handed me my

Soma passport

she emphasized one visit per week

will limit the greedy and the chancers

taking an advantage.

I shop my usual, ZZ the human being

trying to stay alive

ZG the artist in need of brush and canvas

and ZJG the writer in need of a laptop

to publish his books.

ZZ will take a sweet or two thinking

of a friend always there to help

a beautiful woman ripe as a pear

a friendly woman

mother

potential model

and certainly a passionate lover.

Perhaps next time a box of sweets for the

aspiring art curator at the nearby museum.

Who knows she might feature my art in

the future at one of her exhibitions.

I'll look her up and see if she is in the mood

for dancing and I could never worry if she

has a liaison with a boyfriend.

Thanks to her interest I will be motivated

to create works that are different to what

I've done up to this day.

I'll need a Muse for more motivation

for friendship love and an artist's addiction.

And since I had met Elena, I muse: If I had

not taken U4 for two stations into the wrong

direction

I would not have met Elena on the bus to

Heiligenstadt 10:03 – Indeed!

This has to do with the law of causalities and

even more: Fate showing me that she is a

fine person/ human and warm.

What a contrast to B!

But she also has a different set-up

of her initial life.

After five months when she announced

That she's still unmarried

the day when B and I had a bout with

an angry vocabulary

I realized that I had coped better with finding

a foothold in the world of socially wounded

than B had

and Elena had noticed that at once

wondering about B, who behaved one day

friendly

just to be angry the next.

Elena wondered why B was physically emaciated

and I told her that B had lost 25 kg's in the last

six months + besides it's her metabolism and the

strict diet she adheres to due to her nervous state.

B must be angry about herself –

I carry on musing myself and telling Elena in

general why B is this way and why she looks

like a matchstick.

What are you doing? Elena is curious.

I draw and paint preparing for a future exhibition.

Elena seems to be worried about me.

I have been also looking for a laptop

but I can only pay for it next month.

What does the laptop cost? Elena asks me.

Over 700 Euros, I reply. This were fragments

of our last conversation I recalled walking in

the drumming light rain toward the customized

container of the *Soma* close to the four huge

market chain-stores.

At least I could shop for the next two weeks

except bread and cake

I'll get it next week.

Thanks R thanks P I say and wrap up the food

into plastic bags as I need no rain onto it all.

Damned! I'll carry on per pedes and then

I'll wait for the bus.

Did not Amed mention

for a few stops one could risk a free ride?

Besides I may have a free ride now with the

pass from Soma. But never mind.

In fair weather I always walk. It cleanses the

mind and rinses the soul from the heap of

trivial agglomerations B binds into parcels

all week long and dumps it onto the floor

of my mind instead of rolling over and warming

my body up when she feels waves of heat

pulsing through her as she often states

after a sleep-interrupted night

having been attracted to a pale moon

and the ghosts of her past

while she carries on with rituals of irregular

celebration at odd times.

I stick to regular intervals of mine

unless I find myself in a creative phase

with its pulsing groove of producing art

with pen/ pencil/ colouring and musical dance

headphones donned and mobile in my bag

brush in my hand

bending over thick paper

that sucks up the strokes and the pouring

of paint.

Unless Ana appears and touches my body

stirs my soul to still feel the once passionate

merging

falling over each other like two wild cats

in heat.

The 21 days of pilgrimage along the

meandering road of desires' molten lava flow.

This road of shared passion

gelling in our act of unifying

still simmers on and on

and will forever.

Amen.nemA.

Weidling Brook with Elephant Dream

6.

Truth-seeker.

Elegies from a spot called*: Vivenot*

had sneaked up onto my heels

like a newborn puppy

hopping about a new life's enthusiasm

to the smell of my skin

to the being it has chosen

to spend a life in love with.

What has changed since the first time

I've come to the sleepy village

having chosen to dress with the

immaculately laid out vines in

geometrically aligned aisles

along the southern hills opposite to

the thicket of the *Viennese Woods*

filled with musical tales

a gentle breeze that strokes one's cheeks

one who had been missing in the

labyrinth of European-scapes.

Discovering an old flame

what an exciting first meeting

just like making love to a virgin

for the first few times

being a chosen favourite man

one - she said - she would never

forget

one - she would come back to

if she would not have been locked up

by social marriage.

Never mind feelings - society said aloud

sneaky in its coldness -

living on a high shelf

Beverly Hill's style

whatever happens to your soul.

Never mind if you are afraid

to go the way of the artist.

Never mind if you have given up

looking for the truth.

It has died between the sheets

the moment ZG the artist made

love to you for the first time

in your blooming life.

A tear in the portrait of remembrance

of a Muse

tears of Simchi had flown to re-emerge

as a flow of warm tears from ZG's

Greek Muse.

The moment he had felt the first time

a merging of lust/ love/ and desire

her intellectual background calling him

as a voice inside to write down his first

thoughts of his feelings.

This - the personal turning point marked

by the love of Ana/ Alfa/ Aneta.

His turning towards creative arts with

an engagement of his total being.

Ridiculed by his friends and associates

looked upon as going cookoo by his

own spouse.

It's impossible serving two masters

at the same time:

I looked upon this artist called ZG

with an integrated sign of his initials

signing his works of art with.

A serious man who loved to laugh

enjoy the stimulation of some tots

of *Raki* with a fellow artist

a joint to share and tease

stopped by the Greek police and

 playing innocent during a control

for barbiturates/ hemp/ grass/ marijuana

or any other flow of names that people

use from country to country

from continent to continent.

He observes the writer ZZ

the poet with flowing long hair

like a lonely lion in the desert

with his green eyes that flicker

in his tanned face from his

long walks in the sun-filled vineyard

paths to and from the nearest

city.

He sits most of the time at home

in the corner of a kitchenette

and he writes up a poem he conceived

while at a regular walk

struck by sudden inspiration.

Following his beloved role model poet

he has learned to understand

by living his own life shed from

artificial app's of falsified information

running after a life

steeped in crass possession of

impersonal mass productions

goods claimed by his peers

as most fulfilling of a status symbol

THAT'LL BE THE REAL LIFE?

The moment he had lost all his

collections of taped music

printed manuscripts

books about travelling

history art and architecture

his clothes once thought of

being precious with hand made

shoes from Harrods's

furniture from the age of

Queen Victoria that B had bought

he cared just slightly about

but he felt in the pit of his stomach

a heat rising to a furnace of bursting

anger about the loss of his library

including all his books of manuscripts

poetry and creative art - he became ill

lost weight

dehydrated

foaming with his lips at curses

then sliding with a continuous fall

into an abyss of crass poverty.

But he had not yet lost either his

memory

nor his creative spirit

thanks great god of the artistic folk

the ones who are a Dionysian group

of Truth and Pleasure seekers

7.

Dionysian Life.

She browses into the ripped open

kitchen door and shouts:

"It smells like a goat here!"

He has to laugh – "It's the coffee

you've brewed

a dark roast heated up too long".

"Nonsense" – She replies." I wonder

what's next with you?"

She leaves through the continued

Hard-battered door

just to return again and ask him to

empty the dust bin – refuse thrown

into a plastic bag

between the sink and the access door.

No wonder she has a smell of a cat

but the artist in ZZ just frowns at such

a nasal over-sensibility

as if she would imply that he has not

washed his penis and he stinks.

"You can join the animals on a farm

Nearby" – she spits out the words –

"and stink with them."

He laughs out loud but rises to empty

the refuse bags in a rush

just to return to the drawing he works on

enlarging a sketch he had done the day

before: It'll be a second study to a bigger

canvas of 1,6 x 2,0 metres and he'll put

it up in the kitchen marking his domain

like a dog – *Dionysos, the dog with intellect* -

and on top with artistic endeveours.

Today the last of summer holidays at the

end of August.

Time to summarize his own efforts from

April to present and draw the balance:

ZG the artist against ZZ the poet.

But isn't it his art of placing words together

not the same as ZG's Bic rolling over

blank paper

which he fills with watercolour and he

sharpens the objects up with fineliner-tips

a merging of free flowing layering with

a contrast of sharp defined geometry?

The more his spouse shouts abuses and

performs her gross irritating dance

the more ideas with an incongruent web

will appear on his pages

shake his artistic endeveours from tip to

toe as he embraces the truth and truth

will hurt definitely

but the truth challenges to ever new

constellations

ever new amalgamations

of minute depictions from a micro spec

of cosmic dust

as thoughts dive like dew from

leaf to leaf.

And in a moment's crescendo

like a drop of lava into an icy sea

followed by a red-hot rock fall and

the sharp sound of evaporating steam

rising up toward the skies

painting landscapes of inspiring clouds.

The burning up of a human

a torch of pain and passion

the great exhilaration that whines

on a downward spiral to the

disintegration of its measured-out

life.

8.

Abul - Evol.

It's impossible to convince one's spouse

of one's freedom

to consume products marked as BIO

yet it all depends on one's metabolism

so he states while she lives on a diet

stricter than his.

Of course she dislikes the smell of milk

camembert and cream.

However while the weather could not

make-up its mind to settle

Many rained out days began holding back

and finally disappeared.

It's time to take the bus to the station

and board the U-Bahn which partly travels

high up above shops built into the arches

of stone and mortar called viaduct.

A mere fifteen minute ride to Vienna midway

where B shops for cosmetics

while the artist has to schlepp his tired

physical frame to the yellow bank with

its yellow-black emblem

that offers a horrid feeling

thinking of a suppressive past

which has somewhat crystallized with one

of its leftover tentacles

and ZZ had not changed over yet to another

bank he had already considered

although friendly clerk Mel is a woman

ZZ likes as she has helped him in the past

when he needed an account pressed by

circumstantial happenings

where his and his spouse's future hung

in the proverbial thread of a balance.

But since then a different avenue of an

associated mind's garden lay beyond

the gates of the city's core

that had opened up from beyond his ghetto

of an involuntary position in life

separated from remaining family members

and his dearest friends.

He awaits the man who is a friend

but much more encompassing a lost father

an unknown brother

distinct owner of an art shop

who appreciates ZZ's art as he exhibits

his dad's art against oblivion.

one day he might put ZZ into a contact

with his wide range of associates and

friends

the circle of beauties he gathers around

him like in a round dance of his

pleasure principles.

T for Tee/ Teetotaler/ Treasure Seeker

Toastmaster/ Teacher/ Team Tommy

Trusted T/ Number Twenty of the alphabet

in German/ Taff in Greek/ Tamas in

Hungarian –

Multilingual in commerce

Lover Man but not drinking like

C Parker

Professor for his commercial doings.

His friend Luba Abul talks with glowing

eyes like Nefertiti.itititrefeN –

about her language teacher

who loved a woman in the underworld

of a city's egg shaped drainage pipework

connecting the lovers

in an enormous network of unseen routes

below the main streets of the suppressing

upper world

the veins acting as a river upon which

they float in their love boat –

ZZ talks about Romeo and Juliet

some sparks ignite his mind

Prokofjev's music pulsing in his head

touching Luba's sensual string

in spite of her presence for just coffee

but then for some intimate sessions

ZZ would deserve but his friend would

consume.

ZZ asks her to try one tot and

she likes his *barack palinka.*

LUBA-LOVE ABUL-EVOL.

One day he'll meet her

in the underworld channel of love.

9.

WU – Vienna and Surrounds.

From solitude of creative work

in the legacy of the leafy suburb of

WU Wienerwald/ Wu-Wunderbar

Vienna and surrounding Suburbia

into the heart of city life

where great things happen to the

spaces at ART FORUM:

mental confrontations

inert in the art of A Frankl

the taciturn man sitting at Cafe Hawelka

drawing his contemp series of women

with animal heads

animal farm in pictorial scenes

nude Muses around marble top tables

quite an association of thoughts

the artist rendered in the search for

truth - with a slice of *Gugelhupf*

and a cup of fine coffee.

B says: It's more important for ZZ

to write his books than helping her

with daily chores of opening blinds

and the entrance door and window

airing the bedsitter in the mornin'

but ZZ dislikes the damp cold air

just before a cup of Melitta-coffee

and before he feels comfortable in

his daily standard garb.

Never mind B is difficult to deal with

and it's impossible to teach an old dog

new tricks: He - the old dog says:

Prioritize the main ingredients for good time

management relative to the person who

should do the tasks

in accordance with the person's or the

artist's own perspective.

Some look upon T as an egotist

yet laud his pleasant personality and state

that he is a great boss to work for.

Others see him as a successful owner of

a shop for art

derived from his father's artistic legacy

and again others see him as a character

on the stage of city life where the saying

goes: *Das gold'ne Wiener Herz* - The golden

Viennese heart - there are still members of

that tradition

the compassion of city dwellers

who passed on their empathy genes

to the next generation.

There are still many things I want to say

ask and bring to a conclusion.

There are still many things that have

their seat in the first row of the senses.

But as T kisses L - I think of Juliet P

the beautiful dancer and actress

who kissed the artist ZG

an act engineered by his gregarious

friend Dr. E. who's portrait fuses with

the face of his new friend T

And the face of L fuses with the face of

Ana - ZZ's main muse who danced around

him drawing/ writing/ painting - in her

beautiful nude.

Another morning: Friday. Time 7:15.

Soon it's time to leave and teach

Amed some German pronunciation.

Words, Lily, Amed, Mr T, the Poet's Shadow, Muses, and
Familiar Faces

10.

Amed.

While he arrives at *Di Sun's* door

he knocks with his red pen on the

glazed entrance door

waiting for Amed to appear and

open up.

He reads meanwhile in his red

notebook a sketch for his novel

Thrill and Anguish - Quest for a Return

Being here is a part of it and indeed an

enormous part

giving lessons to Amed in German.

Sitting at the black stained wooden table

ZZ observes parents guiding their children

to primary school

its entrance a stone throw opposite

Di Sun's window

as mothers appear in greater numbers

kissing their daughters good-bye

more girls than boys

some fathers with their sons.

Amed serves a plate of Egyptian sweets

prepared with honey and enriched with

pecan nuts - delicious.

He still has to prepare some dough for

pizzas and the lesson will move some

fifteen minutes until he'll be ready.

Amed - industrious but polite in his abrupt

reactions kisses ZZ's cheeks on intuition

and hands his teacher a banknote which

ZZ refuses to take but he insists: You are

like a father - he says softly and places

the note into ZZ's pocket.

It's welcome but ZZ is startled by Amed's
emotions to accept an elderly pensioned-off
artist into his family.
Indeed this slender young man from Egypt
has more love to give than ZZ's own spouse.
His progress in reading German improves
and ZZ will face the challenge to get Amed
prepared for his exam.
Besides he'll take ZZ to Soma while all other
colleagues are still away to avoid bad talk.
Gentleness and love between men are
still discriminated against.
However as ZZ is not gender orientated
he is still glad to help Amed to understand
a 300 page book about the rules of the road
and the way of it being taught in Austria.
It's been extended considerably since the
times ZZ had been doing his driver's exam

60

as it is now done by multiple selection of

the answers provided on a computer screen.

Amed has still difficulty of understanding

and reading the questions in German.

ZZ will make it simpler for him.

ZZ the teacher

who slipped from his artist's skin to help.

Amed is grateful.

Buying yoghurt/ biscuits/ orange juice/ muesli

cheese and rolls/ whole wheat rye bread/ fruit

shopping for 10 bob includes even a poppy seed

cake.

The food will be enough for a 10 day period and

ZZ will be all right.

Most of all he is concerned buying a computer

but his spouse plays up against it lately and

he has to go it alone if she does not agree with

financial help although she agreed before.

But now as ZZ had paid back to Mr T

his personal debt

he has no money left.

B - having been part of that debt to purchase

food for them both - refused to pay half of it

due to her efforts to help dissolve

their back rent for a flat in Athens.

Waiting for the next monthly payment at the

end of September.

ZZ might be in a position to pay for his laptop

purchase with a first instalment.

He is looking forward to place his manuscripts

onto his gadget and send them

electronically to a local publisher he had already

contacted telephonically.

ZZ reads up in his book of Yiddish and he states:

Here lives a mensch. Over his door there's

nothing inscribed but his *mezuzah* is on his

domain on the kitchen wall hung full of his art –

his lucky sentences

his consecration of his temporary home.

T is part of ZZ's *mischpoche* –

his extended family.

Once ZZ joked with Dr. E that all that distinguishes

them physically from another is that his friend

is circumcised. Thus the pun in *The Joys of Yiddish:*

The rabbi gets the fees but it's the *morel* who gets

all the tips.

So ZZ told T when he asked him about his wife:

She always *mutches* me and I already *mutche* along.

11.

Spirit of an Angel.

I am conscious as a *mensch* –

ZZ says and slips from his protagonist-shell.

Those days of a palate's overdrive.

Too much food at once.

The young man from Egypt sinewy built

swung sinuous lips from Pharaonic times

bakes flat breads and composes delicious

delicacies enticing one's senses.

Drawn to men he is probably a dedicated

friend

someone in touch with his feelings/ desires

dreams/ although he had only outed himself

in metaphoric ways

gingerly like a cat on soft paws.

I have slipped into the role of a tutor for

German

a language foreign to us both.

Besides his gender leanings he is keen

to tap any man's homoeroticism and follows

it like a dog the bitches' scent.

But he is in good behaviour following

the rules of his religion

talking social commitment

meaning love he has to give to many.

He feeds his friends and teachers

who have to slow down his acts of

generosity.

The young man who jumped to life

from papyrus scrolls of the Pyramid Texts.

The messenger from antiquity

who signals to me the belief of the

labyrinth's existence

he has envisaged once with only

a secret peek.

I have never believed that meeting people

is sheer coincidence

but on the road of seeking the truth

it often seems a detour from the road

of a desired direction

with something impossible or trivial

an unimportant chat or a *tohuwabohu.*

Yet the poet ZZ opens his eyes and

pricks his ears

as his senses become sensitized like

fine antennas.

Suddenly he stands in front of a mountain

of first-hand information

alive in one messenger sent by his

past Muse

the spirit of an angel

the truth to peek at through a spy hole

on the door to his soul.

At Soul's door.

Welcome.emocleW

12.

Again.

Leave earth's heaviness behind

strut the day with a lightness of being

with art and in the magical process

of creating art –

in the art of a thought-free conscious –

in a consciousness of free thought

with a flight of the soul

leaving gravity of pains of ageing

impossible to return to earth

that has been trashed

not alone with mountains of waste

but mental disasters

ignorance and inhumanities

many callers with a social conscious

weighting will relate to WWIII.

But then you have no intention

of fighting windmills of bureaucracy

with its contradicting jungle of bye-laws

like the growing heap of waste in an

eternal fight to break it down

find humanity's needle

in the planet's haystack again. Again.

AGAIN.NIAGA

13.

Back to Front

The sound of falling chestnuts

bouncing off dark rocks

while the murmuring of the brook

rises and falls like sounds from

the headphone's Rock'n Roll

an incredible not trusted artist's

interpretation of realities

faces like pebbles in still lakes

between man-made weirs

boles placed against huge

unhewn rocks

faces like:

Luba - Love/ Abul - Evol

Prokofjev - vejfokorP

Putz - ztuP

Stup - putS

Pussen – Stuppen –

words like he wishes to collect

for his pending sonnets of

teiluJ & oemoR – Romeo & Juliet

to the sounds and rhythms of the

Weidling brook

along a chestnut-studded promenade

Regibröh - hörbigeR

Nuf - fuN

Gnivol – lovinG

and forever it should be good luck

with it to carry on… carry on.

Like Dema - ameD

Like Ana - anA.

14.

On the ground.

Thrown by circumstance

to the outskirts of one city

rich in culture and deed

to the inclusion of a heap

of people

clambering at a box of steel

and plastic

for some date-expired food

from shops for the well-to-do

readily available on Tue Thu

and Sat's for a few bob

some's pretty good stuff

keeps one alive and going.

Besides a tattooed social helper

feisty woman with a heart of gold

who cares for good coffee and

some experience in the ever

growing world of social underdogs

and under-bitches

and once well-positioned hoboes

for the ruling crowd

whatever…

The artist gives much more than

he'll get to keep him alive

milk him like a buffalo

make him monkey

feed him peanuts as a price –

The bitter song of a Saturday morn'

not entirely desperate for food again

as Amed feeds the artist admiring

his well-toned thighs

but as an artist why not receive

the pound of recognition in lieu

of a pound of meat?

Selfish self-centered wooing crowds

for rap funk jazz-classics in one

dense-stirred pot.

The artist paints and yet nobody

knows

except for a few friends

except for the man of gentle talk

who wears the yellow star of David

still upon his heart.

So the artist bleeds.

So the people still love bread and

games

blood on the carpet.

Saturday. Sabbath. Day of September's

payment

rain and cold

but money to go for

share the money with one's spouse

repay the debt to Tommy

who loves to present the poet as

his son.

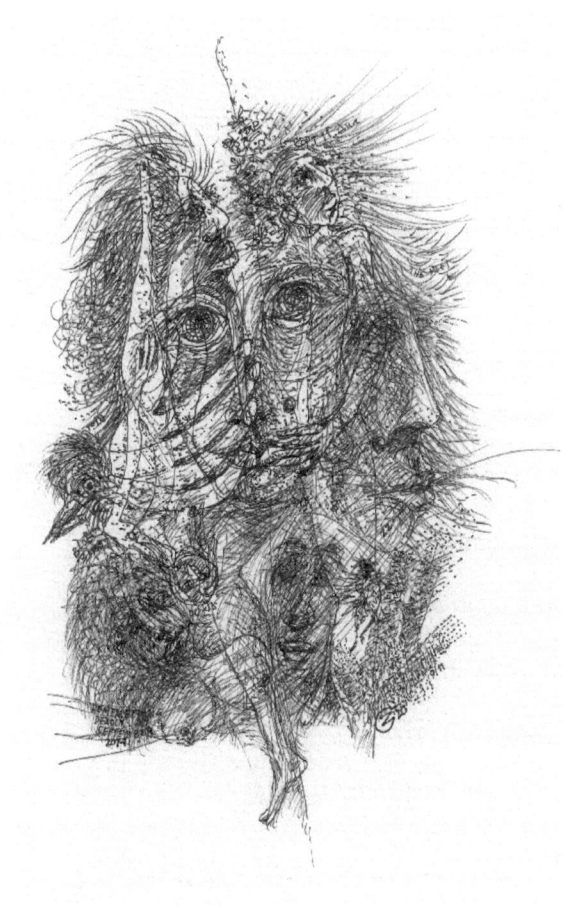

Thoughts about 9/11. Muse A's trip to the Stars

15.

September's End.

Friday evening's earlier darkness

beginning of the blues

arguments about life's present

incompatibilities.

B rolls up her emaciated body

in a temporary bed

covered up in a woolen coat and

in this bedsitter of no other choice

where an early writer's cold and

poverty competes with powerful

bites –

where OE1 plays Mozart's sweet

symphonies through headphones

where rhythmic pop music sounds

for a 45 minute walk

OE3 OE4 as choices of one's mood

all yours.

Passed debates about principles

in married life have long left behind

but flame up festering in a

wounded mind.

The artist paints soft faces

dancing bodies of his muses

and nymphs

against the hard carved face

of a stooped old man.

A long-legged crane's majestic

sculpture

in white against the murky waters

of a gently flowing brook

wings of grey like passing clouds

she takes off toward their passing

of a bitter overflow of fine spray

that etches the skin

and spots the roads

where iron blades of grass cut one

into half

like the memory of a love

she was ripped off at her best age

like prime fruit from a tree of passion

yet it could never been ripped out

from her lover's soul

not if we would have been killed

by the raven's black head of death.

while warm covers hover in the

moist sea of a scented garden

terrace on the Riviera like coastal

comfy settings of Athens's southern

suburbs

even if *Piet* messages me bad news

about my blocked account

in Africa of the South.

And while *Amed* bakes Egyptian food

with delicious round bread decorated

with fish onions like hair

locks browning in red juices

amongst fiery peppers -

how delightful and nourishing to have

a hot dish on a cold shaky midday

in a tightly knit community

at the outskirts of a huge and famous

town of the world.

16.

Cup of *illy* espresso.

No strange vibes or

disturbing noises but stillness

of the blue endless extension

above a rooftop

that shaved off its steep incline

chimney slots have deep-set eyes

and happy rough brick faces.

Molly and her hubby dolled-up

lifted off by stiff breezes

dance like colourful strings

into an endless universe.

But contemp sounds from the

space of headphones in fusion

of songs in a remix fashion

new compositions free from

stringent measures

hourglass figures of sensual muses

sent from an unusual lover

a muse once herself

an interlocutor and best friend

a caring mother   a lost sister

and erotic soulmate

sharing deep layers of consciousness

inaccessible even to one's spouse.

No rushing car's swooshing sounds

channeled like acoustic brickbats

into an angry neighbour's verbal

cacophony.

But a spouse remodeled through

a process of endless purgatory

offers you a hot cup of illy espresso

even without sugar sweet as love

once at the start.

Along the Weidling Brook – The World

17.

Girl from Bangladesh.

Muses lit up bright
faces mingling at the glazed facades
like ants
the entrance beleaguered
students by a busload and
artists amongst the art-happy crowds
a quick walk before the celebratory
speeches will start.
A few artists strike as something new
at least they capture their viewers
and soon bored with it all
ZZ wanders off to see *Frohner's*
expressive art that he appreciates
with its brutality and inert erotic
power
he wanders along driven by thirst
to the underworld of crated art
where he fetches a glass of wine
and some bread
watch a girl with brown eyes
Ana as a young artist.
I leave ZZ at the bar and talk to her
as ZG the artist, who had no luck
to make it into the end phase of
selection for the competition at
this contemporary art event.
I've known you all my life

the girl next door whom I made
laugh the girl next door I lifted up
on a staircase landing
to have a view to the outside world.
She wants to have her photograph
taken with me
the girl next door
I break a glass placed on the floor
I take a selfie and she looks up
my works of art she comments on
the girl next door is like a sister
somebody special indeed
we talk until she wants to leave
I take her to the train
the girl next door does a video
lets me talk about life
I want to see her again and get
to draw her paint her
she lets me paint her while she
talks.
The train arrives and she'll go
with her ticket I asked her to buy
we will be back for more, will we?
The girl from next door
the girl from Bangladesh.

18.

Rini – Inir.

The crated art like in a cryo-lab

conserving the artist's soul forever

I take the pink canvas chair

next to a young dusky woman

say hello to a fellow artist.

Forgotten the dark images

of *Frohner* and *Nitsch* for now

we dance on a wave of soul relations

the eastern flower opens for a sniff

and smells of mystical history

gleaming in her dark brown eyes

the girl the love one muse had sent

me Ana had sent me.

She'll look at my free art and likes

the way I am painting

a process of initial constraints

to be broken down and freed in

free-style painting

just like poetry and writing

on a winding road of self-realization

Orpheus in the underworld

between the labyrinth of boxed-up

art and the endless windings of the

soul.

The 655 artists who submitted the

handprints of their hearts.

I ask for her name - Rini - Inir –

from now on the youngest Muse

in the later phase of my existence.

I fell in love with her eyes.

19.

Skin and Lips.

I told her a story

she activated her Digi-cam -

I want to make a movie - she smiled

pointing her cam at me while we

walk along a city lit up for its

900 year's birthday celebration.

She encourages me to speak:

I am an artist having started out

here

travelled the meridian to the end

of civilization

and found the place where first man

had dwelled

origins of *Alta Mira* derived from the

cave paintings at *Clanwellan* and the

Western Cape

when the thick ice crust had melted

down

man travelled on foot

painted in self-realization

we still do as well

and converses in the cellar like caves

of *Essl*-museum

between conserved art - wooden boxes

in colours, green blue –

while we paint in orange and red

blue and purple and sienna

but then the dust-polluted world

is still our oyster

and I dream of her leg pulled up high

her body covered only by her panties

she'll enjoy the art of hedonism

even if she pours herself over her

huge drawing paper

board

canvas

camera

eyes and ears

skin and lips.

Lovers on Vivenot Lane

20.

Albert.

She tells me her story

of life as an artist

student from a distant

land

dusky-eyed with an open

smile

videos of celebration

a colourful attitude to

her existence

a circle of the chosen

who network on their

mobile gadgets

exhibitions visited

book-signing events

the fleet-footed messengers

of Toth - Hermes -

wing-fitted spirits in their

creative worlds

touching the elderly artist

whose spirit gels with their

potential love-lore

she had also painted

into her portraits

while he has done so in

prophetic anticipation

talking soul-bonding

fingertips across her lips

philosophizing brother: Albert -

collocutor with poetic spirit

the imaginary world of the

artist: ghosting search for the

truth's unique expression

the painter's magical dabs

of colourful emotions

echoing hers: orange - blue -

white and amber -

befitting her warm dusky eyes.

21.

The Musical Stroll

I stroll daily along
the *Weidlingbach*
murmuring its varying
cantatas
viewing the faces
of a host of performers
in monologues about
beauty perceived
at different times
left hurriedly behind.

One of particular
Beautiful face
almond shaped
a lighter shade of a
dusky muse whose
features set against
the pallid marble.

The two muses' gender
dancing moves
come to life again
and a triad of love
the poet's soul
enraptured once.

Why would it float along
bubbling
denuded like liquid glass
and at its natural weir
stir up cast away mirrors
of never ending emotions?

Unzipping the light
from a pole dancing day
a poet's sweet emotions
YOU MUSE raise
continuing between us
for the better of words
for love's gentle art of
instant communication.

And even if I lose my way
in the thicket of the
brook's willows
I'll peg my words of love
into its strands of hair
that stirs its crystal water

and carries my message
toward your body's shore.

However it transforms as
A cycle of Instagrams
sweeping the monitors
of our minds
entertaining our days
of once closeness
without face masks
we wear on empty streets
while the bodies stayed
behind like shell's
décor on the warm sand
of beaches
we've once shared.

Fin

The Poet in the empty Holzkirchnerg. Pedestrian Mall

The Vivenot Elegies

Originating from the first time of the realization of a quest for a return to his homeland, the poet has been inspired by R.M. Rilke's *Duino Elegies*, he read on the laptop of a friend. From a reasonable and affordable life in the South of Africa, he had also endeavoured with some art exhibitions of his creative artistic work in Athens, Greece. Besides, his longing for expressing his innerness in word and with his brush and drawing pens.

He had not intended returning from the natural wonders of exquisite beauty of the landscapes in the Karoo and the moonscape-appearances of Cape Agulhas, also the historically important city framed by Table Mountain and the two contrasting seas of the Atlantic and the Indian Ocean, the breathtakingly undulations along the Southern African beachfronts and the scenic drives along Chapman's Peak. There – a land of contrasts of a natural multitude of fauna and flora, of coloured earth and seas all around its perimeter, semi-deserts and deserts in the western parts.

The legacy of rich decorated cave-walls and the culture of the San-people stayed as inspiration for ZG-the artist's major influence. Back to a Europe in the changing whorl of a melting pot for a new civilization due to a multitude of cultural migration, it offered a new perspective. A trip back from Africa to one's roots, due to political changes that seemed to erode one's professional existence, is never an easy decision, also very hurtful, but a necessary step for personal survival.

Into these contrasting events the basis of poetry and art of the poet and artist has evolved as a healing dressing to the wounds inflicted by barbaric events and unnecessary violation; freedom misunderstood by the masses of uneducated, a great mismanagement of ignorance and neglect of leadership, besides tribal leadership that had refused stubbornly to any change of its chiefdom's dominance.

However, having worked at various projects, including clinics, hospitals and cultural centres for all residents, irrespective of believe and colour, the artist's return to Europe has been disappointing, as having worked as architect in South Africa, meeting with an unsurmountable local bureaucracy as the major hindrance for contributing - with one's experience of 30 years - to local projects.

Into this crass contrast of ability against bureaucracy, the artist's mind had generated an enormous boost for survival. ZJG, the poet has endeavoured to edit his poetry, short stories and novels, and offer them to a German Self-publishing agency for printing on demand. This welcome publishing company has furthered the incentive of the artist to publish his 'oeuvre complete' in due time. These elegies are an outcome of his times of resettlement, together with his spouse, into the countryside atmosphere near Vienna. In the solitude of country life, the artist finds productivity and a welcome change of atmosphere to the city of Vienna, a half-an hourly trip by bus and subway.

While he teaches German to an Egyptian immigrant, he is not surprised of the student's difficulties to integrate into the local society, as most immigrants stick together nurturing their mother-tongue and their customs they were brought up with.

He meets a young woman-artist from Bangladesh at an exhibition in a local museum and they become friends. For some time his art focuses on their common language of artist and Muse. During his repetitive trips to the capital, he experiences the local art scene at the Academy of Fine Arts, where his friend is educated, and she shows him her work in progress that furthers his artistic experiences, while she brushes off her cultural legacy in her interesting work.

Other books by the author
available at the BoD-bookshop:

About the author

Born in Eastern Austria, close to the Hungarian border, he witnessed as a young man the horrors of a nation's suppression, erupting in the Hungarian revolution of 1956.

He finished his education in art and architecture in Vienna, married, and sailed for the Cape of Africa, an adventure that followed his childhood dreams. He had drawn African animals for his art classes, but the time had come to see them in their natural habitat.

Meeting a varied facet of people and cultures, working as a draughtsman in an engineering office, as an architect for a cultural centre, as a coordinator of craftsmen and professionals, he made good use of his language skills traveling throughout Southern Africa.

During a trip to Lesotho, a native artist showed him rock-paintings with their stark palimpsest outlines and with typified movements of animals and humans. It made a lasting impression on him and influenced his artistic work.

His vast collection of drawings and slides had been lost during a change of domiciles, but further studies of the art of the San-people reawakened his dormant artistic longing for expression of his art, filling sketchbooks with drawings and notepads with poetry and prose. While revisiting the capitals of Europe, he sensed the bond of art being borderless and free, reaching out across continents into the world.

During a visit to Greece, he was accepted into a circle of artists and poets, who encouraged him to continue his art and a friend introduced him to the works of famous Greek poets.

In South Africa, he joined writing and poetry workshops of Writers Write. It was to open the floodgates of his creativity.

He decided to travel through Greece and visit its sites of antiquity, read-up on Classical mythology, and to enjoy translations of Greek poetry and prose.

He settled in 2013/14 in Klosterneuburg-Weidling. Poet Nikolaus Lenau is buried here. Franz Kafka had visited here. Their writings will always be an inspiration.